FIRECRACKER

FireCRACKER: A White Guy From Oklahoma Takes On **Systemic Racism / CrackER with a Soft R / Racism with a HARD R.**

Other Books Released By Tyler Lazarus

1. Oddity/ler: Scorpion, Eagle, Phoenix/ Pain, Power, Glory

2. KONG FLU PANDA ☣: <u>The novel virus that went around the world and the geopolitical tensions that came with it</u>

3. KONG FLU PANDA 2 ☢ : DEPOPULATION

ISBN
Fonts by Jess Latham. Thank You.
Printed, Distributed and Bound in the United States of America First Printing
July 2020
Published by He Who Rebels Against All
Oklahoma City, Oklahoma 73106

Hey, Thanks for getting a copy!
Facebook.com/TylerLazarus1992
Facebook.com/Oddityler

ODDITY.LER

Where innovation takes precedence
AUTHOR / INTERNATIONALLY SOLD / SOCIAL SCIENCES

DEFY CONVENTION / THROUGH INVENTION

I WILL NOT SUBMIT TO A MAN

I WILL NOT KNEEL TO THEIR GODS

A QUICK HUDDLE, TO COIN THE TERM

This book was undeniably the most difficult novel to write, over all my published + non-published works.
Because, You know, I was less afraid to take on religion and religious belief, than I was to tackle RACE and RACISM.

Simply because, the myriad mental experiences that we, as people, have towards ourselves and others are highly intricate AND complicated and to pull apart that "web" of belief, was TEN times thicker than the sticky consistency of religious/spiritual webs that run throughout the human brain.

Of God, Heaven and "continuing" on after THIS - that's one thing - but stepping into the MINEFIELD of prejudices, unspoken assumptions, strongly felt dislikes towards other individuals of different colors and backgrounds, I didn't know if my skills of both observation and articulation were quite ready to synthesize SUCH an issue.

Everyone **FEELS** themselves capable of taking on the topic, and adding their two cents into this conversation, but that's all it ends up being - 2 measly, forgotten cents - we need a thousand dollar bill to really CHANGE things.

The new thousand dollar bill doesn't yet exist,
but I'm going to help create it.

FireCRACKER: A White Guy in Oklahoma Tackles Systemic **Racism**

AKA DUALITY/LER
The Sequel to Oddity/ler

Winks

Meditating on top of a mountain
OHM
Breathes in *INHALES*
Camera sees a "monk" from the back
Suddenly turns and checks Apple watch as birds chirp from up high

It's hot, and it's about that time to leave.
I think, to myself.

Flings prayer beads off and rips off orange monk shroud, revealing Versace
pants and a custom, colorful blazer

Walks down the rocky path and gets into a Black Lamborghini

Shuts doors Revs the beast of an masterful engine

Shifts into third gear
Aggressively Speeds off

*Diana Ross, *Do You Know Where You're Going* Plays and fades off into the
distance*

♪ ♪ ♪ 𝄞

The radio stations quits playing happy pop music and fades into an announcer saying to take precautions this week as Corona Cases are skyrocketing and now there are **478,000 dead**, and 9,295,000 infected.

I remember when there was only *14,000 dead.*

Pause the protests

Pause some white lady writing "but all lives matter."

Rewind time
The city skyscrapers build down, they speed back and cars become horse and carriages
The city we know becomes an open field
Lightning flashes and the sky changes again and again
Rain falls

First, there was slavery.

White man cruelly whipping a black man
Black man answering in a yelp of pain and [forced] obedience

An ugly ugly UGLY historical truth and snapshot
Envisioned in our collective minds

Slavery first, THEN COMES segregation

Whites only, blacks to the very back
No blacks allowed

Dr. King gives a speech on the town steps but is muted by time moving so fast

Justice ... for all????
Freedom.... for all?

Pause again, rewind again
Back to the days of EL slavery

General granger goes down to Texas to deliver the final news and choice that slavery
has ended - forever- after the emancipation proclamation

Juneteenth, July fourth
Aunt Jamaima, uncle Ben
Uncle toms cabin and Uncle Sam

Here's the ugly truth of a (nelson) mandala of ugly truths
White people refused to acknowledge slavery had ended
White people Keeping their slaves in the dark
About the new freedom in Texas for two years
Until forcefully pushed to surrender their slaves as freemen and free women
With unalienable rights of their own

So let's put it together

Slavery, segregation, black lives matter

BLM is really the third concussive shockwave to the system of slavery
in the fight for equality
And what a fight it's been

The fight didn't stop in the country fields of the civil war
As soldier lay dying in agony with soldier

White people fighting other white people
About black people

Has anything changed?

In 1862 to 2020.

I walk into the post office to pick up my

Delivery orders

It's during covid 19 so only three people can be inside at any time so that means two customers and one worker

The ladies , the worker and the customer, are both black and I'm waiting back as she's finishing up shipping her items and she asks the lady "hey, have you tried that snow cone place around the corner.... it's so good! I actually need to get some change so I can go over there after this, can you break a five down into quarters for me?"

The worker says yeah she can and she hasn't tried the snow cone shop,
She asks the woman what it's called.

"It's uh,.... it's called.... damn, I can't remember the name now that you've asked me."

She laughs, still trying to remember

Do You mean ******* ? I ask out from behind them

YES, she says excitedly that's it!!!!

Yeah it's called *********

She turns to me and smiles and I laugh saying how good all their stuff is and she busts out laughing going I KNOW, I'm addicted to them

So the worker is finishing breaking down her change and we're talking about our favorite flavors and the worker says she doesn't like anything too sweet because it messes with her stomach and both me and the lady tell her to try such and such if she doesn't want something too strong

Mind ü, this is all during race riots and racial tension with shops being broken into and destroyed on live channel nine news the very night before with white people and black people yelling at each other and at police and everyone cussing up a storm of rage, pent up during the last 100 years.

She gets her change and tells the postal worker to be sure and try them when she can and laughs with a remark that she can't believe she lives and works on this side of town and hasn't been over there

The lady and I both laughed redoubling our praise of the snow-cone stand and why she MUST try it during the scorching days of summer

She waves goodbye as I walk up and ask the postal worker to check the back room for any inventory that's arrived this morning with my postal box number to pick up new orders to send out to customers for my books

She tells me she'll be just a minute and disappears

I'm waiting in the cool and quiet mail room, as the fan whirls around, half broken.

As the original lady runs back in laughing up a storm and tells me she can't find her phone and she thinks she might have put it inside the box she just shipped

I cackle looking for the package to see if we can reach and tell her I'll call her. We both peer over the counter to see if the box vibrates or we get any sign of it inside

I pull out my phone and she tells me she's gonna go check her car real fast to see if it's there first

She disappears out the front door as the mailroom attendant comes back and tells me nothing arrived yet for orders and I've got the phone up to my ear laughing now myself and I tell her the snowcone lady lost her phone and thinks it's in the shipping package but she went outside

My phone is still ringing as the attendant busts out laughing and runs over to the box
and shakes it gently and listens

While we wait, in silence together, listening, the first girl comes bolting back inside
and answers the phone at the same time saying IVE GOT IT with a smile on her face

All of us laugh and she looks relieved that she didn't just mail her phone over to
Tennessee to a relative, as the attendant and I are giggling at the exchange of events
from snow cones to missing cellular devices within ten minutes of time around each
other

The lady says goodbye to us and texts me from her car thank you with a heart for
doing that
And I reply with some emojis and the pink heart sign and wish her well and good luck
and also to get a good snow one

That's how it should always be

No white person trying to act black
No white person trying to be extra to make black people feel "comfortable" - - - -
Which only makes black people feel ridiculed and ridiculous

It was a human moment between us three where skin color wasn't even a factor or a
thought or even a visual cue to hate each other

The world was outside fighting each other
And we were inside truly seeing each other
Not as a gay person
Not as a black person
Not as a white person
Not as a religious or WHATEVER person

We were just three people in a little mail shop together
Passing time with laughter on this complicated little space rock
Going around the sun

No angry cops
No protest signs
No chants
No yelling from large crowds
No graffiti
No broken windows
No burnt and busted stores

Just a trio wishing each other well
Unconsciously and unspoken tenderness
On their journey of this life

That's a real moment of shining humanity
That isn't dramatic over the top
Underhanded
Done for kudos
Accomplished in front of a camera, a selfie
No virtue signaling
No ten thousand likes and a photo with us
No literary embellishment or scenario
Added only for allegorical emphasis

A
Quiet
Perfect
H U M A N
Experience

That's what real human interactions look like.
Or should look like

And there were clear differences between us if you're wondering
Writing a real scenario sounds so whitewashed and vanilla on black and
white paper
They sounded black _ not Caucasian Karen's
And I sound gay - not straight gym chads
There are auditory and visual differences
This world is not a homogenized entity of TOM AND SHEILA

Of white male robots eating puss-ay disguised as gentlemen
I know that's what has turned the world until now
But I think what turns it going forward
Will be a mixed bag of things
And not just black or white thinking

We may have to go TO extremes to solve these issues
 But extremism is not going to solve any issue

Radical anarchy is a fools paradise to solving societal issues
When you destroy a business and burn it down
Realize in your limited thinking
Tha5 THAT building could have belonged to a black owner

Black lives matter
But also those lives THAT are connected to the property they own

We have ended slavery
But we have not escaped it

It's now financial and not personal

It's not Aunt Jemima, or Uncle Ben..
not even Uncle Tom's Cabin…

Baby, it's always been about Uncle Sam.

Do you think ANYONE>???? cares whether we bust our asses and still
don't have enough for rent
Do you think our landlord gives a shit
Shit the wording itself is medieval and evil l.m.a.o.

Nobody cares about ü and I
As everyone is focused on climbing to the top
And out of lower class hell

Make no mistake
This existence - despite safe zones and soft unicorn people
Is hellish

This life is such a struggle
On emotional, psychological, financial fronts
This life can be so tough ---
That people end up taking their own lives

This place is super fucked up
Never forget that fact

Because it's a self evident one.
Hidden behind all of our smiles and laughter.

As East meets west,
400,000 people die

它来自我们

429,666 to be exact as it continues to sky rocket
Half a million

A map of the United States showing every state touched by the virus
from the East
As another map overlay shows the states where racial tension has
exploded
Little red dots of the virus on one panel
And little green dots on another

One represents death and pestilence
The other represents frustration rage and anger

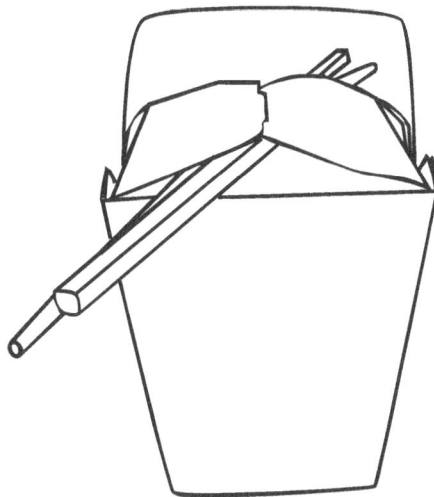

Yin of China
Yang of America
The year
20 (TWENTY)
20 (TWENTY)

There's been a LOT that's transpired this year.
Obviously, nobody would put out FOUR books in 4 quarter period, unless
a lot of complicated, cultural pieces were moving at the same.
It starts with Kobe Bryant going down in flames, inside a helicopter,
Australia catching on Fire, China unleashing a vile new biosample on the
world, whether purposely or not, and Black and White people goinG at IT
back in the Western Mainland.

HOT AIR

Black lives matter
And so does the business connected to those lives and the lives of
others
AGAIN -
Life matters, and so does the businesses keeping THOSE lives alive

A map of dots showing covid sickness
A map of dots showing protests against racism, worldwide

This is a tipping point it's no longer just America's sequestered problem
of white vs blac but the spoken tension of all black people across the
world

Silent spreading virus
Spread FROM air particles
Loud angry spitting vocalizations in the street
What could possibly go wrong lmao

我们做到了

For four months Americans are isolated inside
And then suddenly rush to go outside
Not because the virus is gone
But because of a new issue now taking their attention
... and the virus keeps spreading

One mans death starts off a Chain reaction
Not seen since Jesus Christ hImself
8 million infected with covid

Shops explode with fire from protesters
Other business close down again from covid exposure
These two elements working at the same time
Is quite something to see in real time

Let's talk about time for a second

— eventually there will come a vaccine for this after all the death
And eventually new measures will come forward, comma collectively,
comma

它来自中国

Lmao but until then dot dot dot... it's a god damn mess down here
Unorganized but people doing their best to go on as normal as conditions
are completely abnormal lmao

I'm stuck in the middle of the mid west wishing I could get the hell out of
dodge

Im taking a little boat back to Europe....

not to be surrounded by white people,
but to be in a society where at least they have their shit together... well
sort of, Europe is trying to Break away from The European Union (In
BREXIT) and has migrant problems with high crime rate sooooo.... IDK.... no
where in particular looks A-M-A-ZING right now lmao.

This place is just ghetttttttto lmao
Oh and they are doing away and defunding the police in certain areas
because of the tensions of police brutality, police injustice and other acts
of aggression they have committed

Fair enough ...sort of... kind o....f...uh.... but not really
They want a new police force to community based to handle threat
escalations
But it just doesn't seem realistic lmao

Nice idea
But yeah these streets are bad

Karla with the [barely hidden] bulletproof vest and a shaky hand on a
pistol is not going to solve the crime problem lmao

Meanwhile, Trump is tweeting that the Supreme Court Apparently hates him

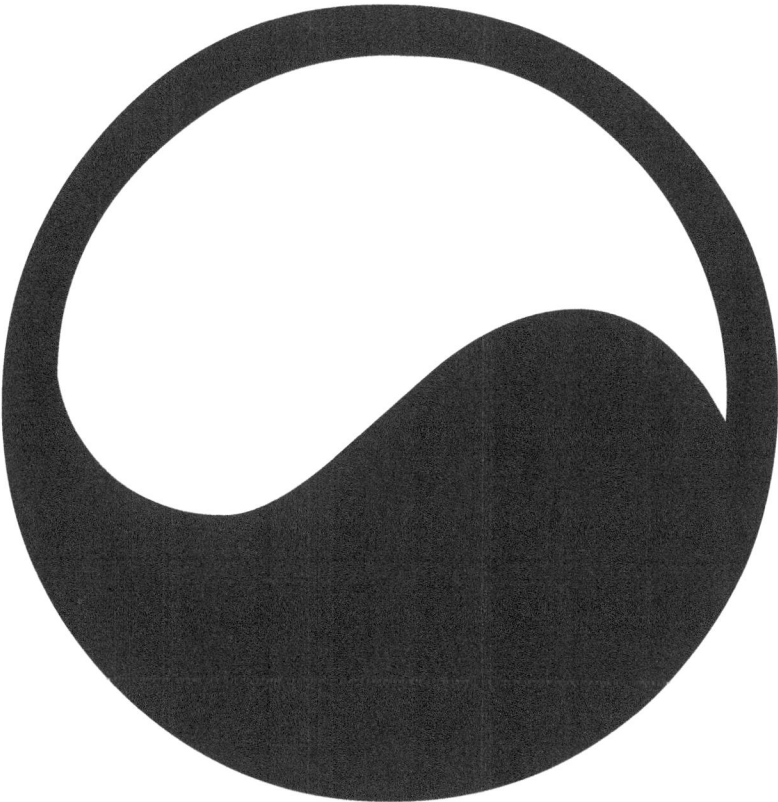

Back to real time

My coffee guy I occasionally flirt with
And I'll deny it's him if he ever reads this
And I know you're married and it's not gonna stop me

He's black and I'm gay
And he goes if I could just not exist in this dimension for awhile
And I'm thinking
If I could get out of this body

This defective dumb gay machine
Well I'm intelligent
But the experience of homosexuality I've experienced has just been
dumb
Not the fun masculine accepted kind of ghey
But the feminine
Squeaky voice
With a soul darker than satan
It's a mismatch lmao

We both wanted out of this reality - For a second
Staring in different directions, half serious
For different reasons

A moment of truth
As his coworkers continue hastily placing coffee orders
And repeating how much Starbucks venti they want
As we both stare at the sky
And back at each other

IN A CHILLY/FEVER DREAM

Sees god
Stares at the stupid, middle-eastern creator of all things

Runs forward and starts throwing a tantrum
Slaps Jesus, angrily

How could you
How could you put me down here with all these people
These confused and deranged nut jobs
How could you do this to me
Put me inside ....a DYING body
And throw me into confusion and historical insanity

starts crying

You put me on a little space rock - getting cooked by a star -with people
who had a war over skin coloring
Dear god why!
Why did you do this to me!!???????????
You put me on a fucking rotating ROCK/orb where people quoted
 nonsense verses THEY WROTE while dehydrated in the desert
And told me I was going to burn in fire
Just because I didn't like girls
The only other gender combination

God stares forward like a cold, unmoving statue
With its eyes lit up

These people are fucking crazy
I want out get me off this planet
Send a car crash my way
Get me out of this body
I don't wanna be down here among them anymore

God still stares unmoving, unblinking, unbreathing

Throws spiritual body against the stone of god

God damnit!

Give me a sign
Just Give me something ...

...A pen falls out and rolls across the floor

Oh come on!
I don't wanna fucking write anymore

Laughs hysterically

"God" transforms into a Hebrew letter - floating in the air -on fire
the very crackling of the form smoldering into ashes as it burns
Then Mohammed
Then an elephant rollerskating
Then shiva, then a many faced angel with an orange veil
Then a gold, broken Scimitar
Then Alanis morrisette passionately playing the guitar, naked
And finally a ball of yarn inside jell-o falling into a black hole
Before it disappears out of sight
Stretched to infinity

Bye god

Back on earth
500,000 people have been killed in a single second
Hello covid urns

它杀死了肺

Im real sorry folks that I'm not giving you escapist Fiction to escape disappear vanish out of reality from

I remember that's why I used to read because my Immediate environment was soooo (intellectually) intolerable that I wanted out of it so opening up a book was my way out.

Suddenly Im Hermione Granger.
Suddenly Im Voldermort.
Suddenly the Koons is Me.

ARTPOP

For Hours, I could build up to complex characters destroying a dragon or some fantastical obstacle lmao

Then as a writer I end up skydiving down into reality
And taking a magnifying glass with me as I descend
From the perspective of airy detachment

I read fiction…. And weirdly write non fiction

I don't care about plot pacing and magic dragons
I care about why are people SO fucking stupid

And I mean that with love lmao

undoes my face mask

blows Covid kisses

Becoming a writer was less of a calling
And a simply a way to call OUT bullSHIT

REST IN PEACE B. TAYLOR
REST IN PEACE G. FLOYD

It starts with a virus from Chinese people
That spreads to all people
Then it hits the white people
Who end up in a clash with black people
As the Chinese people remain SUSPICIOUSLY silent
And let the white and black people fight
While the Beijing People Fade out as the drama begins
Then other people, more people get involved
Gay people come out of the woodwork because this mess is happening in June
Which coincides with Juneteenth for black people
And further resentment begins from white people
Who have had issue issue in the past with gay people
Disagreements from other straight people
Intense infighting between other homosexual people
And Christian people

31,276 Dead in NYC from COVID-19
2,977 Died in NYC from 9/11

Meanwhile to the north, kinder white people
Also known as Canadians
Go about their Caucasian business
While to the south
Mexican people ARE
Considering building
A WALL - to protect themselves - from the very white people
That tried to build a wall against them lmao

Brazilian and South American people
Dying in droves
Having to set their own people in makeshift f7nerals on fire
Because of the dense population city dynamics
Causing more and more people to die from covid

A youtuber passes away after the corona virus causes meningitis, and
his condition worsens until he is GAME OVER screened.

French people
German people
Iranian people
Shades of other white people
Tan people
Darker people

All of the people living life in not peace. But intense and personal
inequalities
All these people in different time zones speaking different languages
Believing in different gods
Believing in different concepts of right and wrong

And all believing themselves to be good and others as bad

Some people on social media posting videos
Some people posting feel good posts
Some outside filming themselves for Snapchat

Some doing lines of cocaine in front of their friends
Some doing TikTok challenges

If America falls because of a bomb
Social media was a global forum that was digital
Posts were information parcels shared on those forums
Snapchat was a platform to record and share filmed experiences
Cocaine is... you can find that one out by your own research
And tiktok is where boredom went to die a slow death by irrelevant
humor
Youtube is where an amusing white woman named Trisha Paytas had
EMOTIONAL meltdowns on the kitchen floor, and ate Fast Food in front of
a cheap camera and made... Millions.

Moving on lmao

There's so much weirdness to all this
Ancient uncivil wounds of American Society
Civil war cannon blasts
And apple TECH loading screens happening at the same time

I'm literally having historical vertigo

swirls head around while taking a shot of tequila

SLAMS SHOT GLASS DOWN

Why did I have to be alive during all these monumental changes and transitions
into the future Because GOD BUHLESS

UH_MARE-RICKAH, llll----LLLand that EYEEE looooooove

misses all the notes

WAS Gay but didn't get to enjoy being gay because of the religious scarification
that greatly reduced the quality of my life as all these new homos get to hold
hands and get married and kiss and Instagram instagay #hashtag themselves to
death
With their matching boyfriend and their stupid little dogs LOL

Race tension going back sixty years suddenly coming back from the dead
As the older generation holds firmly onto their ignorance of black people and
differences and the newer generations are left confused and cartwheeling in
anger because they don't understand it's the older folks still clinging to outdated
belief systems
Creating systematic racism

Don't get me wrong
There is white privilege still existing in whitey-titey Whites from wealth and
affluence shielded from all the harsh realities
But if you're white and Had no wealth no hand up or hand out
Please keep your hands safely in the ride for the remainder
In the country where we have the right to bare arms
And come from the poorhouse

That privilege just ain't the same
Ok but I'm not going to compare white privilege dicks
In a poverty pissing contest with other whites or blacks lmao

Or any other people

I came from nothing and have barely managed to be middle class after a life of
quiet desperation to amount to something and even with books sold across the

goddamn globe Lmao

For fucks sake is about all I have to say
wipes brow of sweat
It takes a lot to amount to more than a hill of cold bbq beans in this #dumb life,
please re-tweet

I haven't even gotten to my own ridiculous ~~fucked up~~ life
This is just the trauma of the collective playing itself out

This is the fucked up nature of other humans
My story has yet to be told and it's not the time to tell it

Presses play on TV screen as riots continue on

BLACK LIVES --- lady needs air after shouting in the same spot for so long --
MATTER

She starts repeating it, faster, and faster and FASTER

As some random white person is in tears retorting back

"ALL LIVES MATTER"

BLACK LIVES MATTER!!! --- cuts right over the white person

White Tears Resume.

Lmao.

Writing oddity/ler was easy. I just had to tell people why I couldn't get
erections for women to finally make sense of homosexuality and the
historical confusion

I can't get a boner looking at a lady - pretty straightforward but still
HIGHLY uncomfortable in daily conversation where people are more
comfortable speaking on the weather's condensation probabilities -

instead of the direction of your erection…. RIP

Book two (KONG FLU PANDA, BITCH) was an emerging virus without absolute dubious Chinese origins moving so fast that I could barely keep up. It took all the might of my mind to maintain that degree of journalistic speed to both sift through information and find the false from the true, as history was being written and consecutively re-written in the same segments of expression.

我们知道是谁做的

Book three. the follow up. was closure and final data amended into the novel virus that swept the globe… still fairly easy stuff to report and write.

Read the news, Dig deep into the Internet, Fact Check, Cross Check, Cross Dress, Drink, Print, Publish, Yeehaw, Celebrate.

Throws Black Cowboy hat into the air

Book four is a challenge in a way the others aren't not just because I've established a reputation for myself and seen my books picked up by stores websites and been sold all the way to China and Australia but because the race issue is hundreds of years old

Well homosexuality is thousands of years old so why the difference.

Not cut out for the job???? CANT DO IT???
WHATS WRONG>????

Because homosexuality - you stupid, fucking idiots - once you understand my wiener can't get hard and stand up - all the Bible verses fall away

It's fairly straightforward even though it's about being gay

Race and being white and black have infinite experiences
Gay men while all different and all along the scale of masc to feminine share the E X A C T same fact that their dicks get hard for guys.

It's a common denominator I can tap into.
Sausage wont get long for a woman's taco.

EASY PEASY LEMON SEMEN SQUEEZY

I knew by the end of book one I had written proof so airtight nobody could argue against it - a cock is simply gonna prick UP for what turns it on - can't fight it

files my nails with a smug expression and hair curlers

I knew by book two and three that I had uncovered a set of conversations so implicative of maliciousness that there were some obvious truth to them NO MATTER how many people said the facts were wrong or lying

I wrote those books not because I was wanting fame or infamy but because I knew i could let the record reflect the truth once I guided the sheep into the pen like an energetic farm dog
I could make a clear difference on those issues

With race,
There is no clear sided victory to be had

Plays the harp as people continue to fight each other

plucks the strings, almost violently

fingers bleed as white and black people continue misunderstanding each other

Smears the blood across the harp strings in a quick pull of notes

互相打架

I'm really Harping on Race, aren't I

RAISES ONE GREEN EYEBROW, GET IT??

There's no set of statements no matter how unifying or divisive that can be said to balance the weight and keep both sides white and black balanced.

Straight people thought that homosexuality had to do with "the devil" BOBBY BOO-SHAE or sin, It has to do with my hairy nuts and mushroom head hotdog, SON.

Waterboy with Watersports, With The Aquarius Watercarrier.

bangs drums

Looks at audience to see if anyone caught ALL those references

whips wig and stares back at the camera

The proof - of gayness - is in the penile pudding.

ITS NOT THE RAINBOW ITS THE COCKAMOLE SHOOTIN OUT ROPES OF PROTEIN GAUCAMOLE

ITS THE PEE PEE

Straight people are beginning to understand gay people, or at least gay guys.

I can't speak for lesbos BUT if I was one, what a nice situation with two ladies.

Men are little fucking horny devils, imagine coming home to someone who is emotionally nurturing, warm and caring, Instead of a Guy Telling you to "lick his balls."

Ugh, so crass.

Honestly, liking women would be so much EASIER, despite the hidden drama they bring, if I could be straight I would lmao.

BUT BACK TO BLACK AND WHITE ISSUES
OF BLACK AND WHITE PEOPLE...

I see evilness on both sides too strongly to be out in the streets marching with black people
Or to be agreeing with white ignorance

I see black lives matter posts
But then read during the middle of all of this that Chicago has its worst day of crime in 60 years with black on black crime

Does a black persons life only matter if a white man takes it?

I see the all lives matter posts and have to laugh
Of course all lives matter (in a terrestrial way but 7nfortunately not a cosmic way)
But it's like black people are suffering an injustice don't make this about you

Black lives have to start mattering or you're gonna have these angry ballistic cops continuing to act completely out of line and bringing down force one thousand plus FIVE times not needed

Black lives matter highlights an issue and I get that

White people, stop it lmao

ALL LIVES CANNOT MATTER
if Black lives DONT matter.

SEE? It's simple.

With that being said not a single social media post of the black lives taken by other black lives

Not one outrage
Not one collective tear
Not even a "WE WILL MISS U"

ROFL…. like??????
How sad
But how fitting to humanity and it's VERY #selective hypocrisy

The absolute brass white people had to enslave another group
Keep them as workhorses inside their plantation houses
 Commonly Treat them with cruelty, coldness and subhuman STANDARDS….

White people created this mess there's no doubt about it
But it wasn't this generation of people

That's the problem
A historical echo is still playing

It's no longer about just skin color
It's about the perceived behavior of people with that skin color
Another epidermal layer of sociological complexity has thickened over
the whipped wounds of slavery

But I didn't enslave anyone
And you did not build the Arby's down the road

So where do we stand here lmao
Don't hold your breath for an apology
I didn't wanna be born into this earthly shithole lmao

(Honestly, who the fuck sent me to this place???
Was I a Fed-Ex package meant for somewhere else??

THERE IS NO WAY I SHOULD HAVE ENDED UP ON EARTH.

I don't owe anyone - anything
And I don't even owe them my time
I don't even owe an explanation

Not to whites or blacks

I think you all are stupid.
Collectively
Individually, SURE, I love the hell out of people
But put them in a group where they play the victim card white people
Or the race card, black people and I'm flipping the whole poker table off

Let the chips fall where they may

只有中国才重要

Blackjack
Hit the road jack
AND JILL
ALL OF YOU Must GO LOL

I'm writing a novel on an iPad while I'm watching people throw Molotov cockatails into structures and a malaria like virus is killing everybody as they cough themselves to #death

This is absolutely ridiculous lmao

Who wrote the plot of this year?
Are we being punk'd??? ASHTON??????

Am I dead???
Am I in hell and just don't know it? Lmao

pushes tired eyes together
I've seen too much on this stupid space rock floating
93 million miles out from a hostile solar bomb

Watches the race riots as protestors hoist signs into the air
As chants of life mattering for those of a skin pigmentation are yelled

takes a bunch of edible gummies

(Was he glorifying drug/substance use here, or was he really just getting high with no shock value???? Literary scholars still cant decide*)

Dissociates from reality
Appears in the middle of the protest as a phantom
Nobody notices or sees as they advance forward like pawns across a chess board

Why am I down here.

What the hell is this place

Looks in both directions

Why is reality so retarded

Yes I said retarded

(Social justice editors scream, YOU CANT SAY THAT.

Bitch, I just FUCKING did)

This is retarded. IM NOT TALKING ABOUT A SPECIAL PERSON

You know when someone says "That's gay…"
and some PREDICTABLE person goes "YOU SHOULDN'T SAY THAT!!!!!! EX-
CLA-MATION MARK!!!!"

Bitch, saying something is gay does not mean its homosexual.

I say "That's fucking gay" all the time - referring to a situation that's simply
STUPID.

Words, have multiple meanings, wrapped in the dualistic syntax of English and
Any other languages Vocabulary.

Chicken Fried Rice does NOT mean a Chicken Fried This Rice

STOP BE-AN OFF-IND-DEAD BY STUPID WORDS
AND START GETTING MAD AT HOW MESSD UP PEOPLE ACT.

We're all constantly standing / existing / living / breathing under
different points of social inequality because we live in a hierarchy and
very rarely is the hierarchy of needs met for everyone person in
capitalism's [designed] situational selfishness.

The person reading this could have come from wealth, status and money
and be richer than us both but say their psychological needs weren't met
then you would be standing on higher ground emotionally than they are
even though they have the gold bag

However, because the gold bag is the true bag to secure inside the

system of capitalism, even if they are suicidal, depressed and unhappy - they still have MONEY, HONEY. They still Possess the keys to opening the doors in American life even if they are suffering internally
And I'm not discrediting from any rich person's mental state

... but imagine being depressed, unhappy, rejected, without familial structure AND POOR.

You would have a HELL of a time TRYING to make it in this life.

I didn't say make it.
I said - TRYING to MAKE IT.

The system is everything
Your immune system keeps you healthy.
The broken healthcare system is what stops all of us from receiving care and instead getting a whopping 90k bill.
The respiratory system is what keeps us breathing
Without that system - and 50 other bodily systems - working together, we would die.

draws on a whiteboard, thudding the black letters together

THE SYSTEM.

keeps writing

IS. EVERYTHING.

FOR EXAMPLE: The solar system is the eight planets and one star keeping it all spinning

The system is everything, caps
An improper system poorly functioning like so many human systems, including bodily, material and physical and financial - prevent life from living properly

A poor system means survival - if that - and not thriving. It's impossible to thrive when a system is designed to be against you

You will grit your teeth and survive but it will not be a happy existence

The system or should I really say, the environment plays a ginormous role on the quality of life and how it impacts the individual and individuals

These same white people scoring hundreds of likes up on social media with posts like "it's important to irritate your white friends if it means saving a black life"

I agree!

Except these were the same white people saying
"If a black table walks in, don't give it to me"
As restaurant staff
Because this one demographic is notorious for not tipping and trying to get free food plus discounts by making a restaurant bend over backwards

Not a stereotype it's just how it's been since the dawn or chicken parmigiana and eggplant.
But I'm not here to elaborate on the quiet nuances of restaurant drama lmao
I'm here to point out the glaring hypocrisy from these same white people acting like the new Martin Luther king jr for brownie points for brown people.
Lmao

Here's the thing, I'm not gonna hold someone's poor wording and racist comments over them forever, people are allowed to grow and change and become different people from that FIRST moment
But these same people, when in the actual heat of the moment, are more apt to repeat the same series of events, wording and BEHAVIORS.

The push for tolerance is more than words
And yes that works both ways, having a group of people try and complain

just for the ulterior motive of getting an entire free meal is also incredibly disappointing no matter the skin color it just happens to be prominent behavior from one group which is what reinforces racial bias no matter how ugly that truth is

Treat people like crap and demand favors and those people are likely you treat you like crap, back

Respect IS a two way street

Switch gears
HEY!! BUT that's not me!
A black person says, with a megaphone.

I don't do that stuff!
I've never done that stuff???
How is that fair??

Baby, it's not
And I went through the same glaring anger at the world

<u>The individual ends up paying the price for the collective</u>

Because people perceived homosexuals AS promiscuous, carriers of AIDS, and just innately #dirty...
I had to live with all my interactions tainted with that kind of filth even though I was spotless of all the charges and beliefs leveled my way

It WASNT fair
Because other gay men had gotten away with acting like filthy swine, I had been charged with the same thing

If other people see a repeat of the same behavior ENOUGH times, that behavior gets engrained into the brain as TRUTH - even if it's not - and then that behavior gets covered like an aura of social stereotypes around that group in question

I hadn't slept around like other ghey males did, didn't hook up, was silently disgusted with gay apps, but my good behavior didn't change a thing. I still had the cross to carry even though I shouldn't have had to move the goddamn thing

Life is NOT fair
Standing at different points of inequality
Let's discuss what that really means

Harvard won't save us
Yale won't save us
Gucci won't save us
Inclusivity And Affirmative Action Wont save us
Overpriced corporate branding worn save us

This is about emotion and empathy, baby
Harvard is studying what that means
But studying is not the same as creating

looks at everyone with severe disapproval

Y'all really had an entire WAR over skin color

A

WAR .....

A WHOLE….. ASS….. WAR.
OVER SKIN COLORS……

A WAR……………………..

中国第一，美国可能受苦

adjusts monocle

A riot is an OUTWARD sociological reaction towards something unjust or conditions that are unfair and wrong - that everyone recognizes - whether they're admit it or not

For every 1000 idiots destroying property
There was only 1 or 2 sane people
Most people's contribution is a reactionary act of destruction. Their entire move towards a movement is anger based

A protest is always more than a protest
It allows people to take their misery and anger of their own lives and make it about something else, for a moment in time

I actively alienated white people by being TOO vocal about black rights ... then to have white people turn around, years later, and tell me I was being too quiet...

Talm….. bout some motha fuckin white

silence

Bitch....

Y'all bout to never see my white ass again

Kiss it

Under all three categories of watching eyes ????????
Curious indifferent and some quietly malicious
I'll find the words and find the way
To liberate my mind
Inside this form and body
(Rip it open)
Technological elixir
Bottled from Atlantis
(Don't bottle all those emotions up)
Volcano of freedom
Erupting out blasphemy
Against these people and their gods
And pure ethical lawlessness
Another shiny psychological gem to add with my initials
Carved and spinning

Clutched TIGHTLY
In the claustrophobic talons of time,
I found myself
Now I find myself without a lover or any private support
But look who is outshining them all
Book after book, image after image
Burning through my star
A lighthouse
Blazes up into a powerhouse
Parts of me in pain

But parts still feel immortal

There is an ecstasy in me that no critic can touch or take away.
They wanna see me fail
I wanna see them reach this level.
laughs
These bitches couldn't even put their boots on the mountain without slipping
And their 10,000 followers won't catch them
I don't wanna be bitter but sometimes ü gotta let them know
That You understand exactly what their silence means
_And that you're watching them
As they're watching ü

SODOMITE WITH THE DYNAMITE / WITH A BLONDE WIG/ TONIGHT, I'LL B

THE BLONDE BOMBSHELL FREE MAN WITH A FREE STYLE

BUT Do ü wonder why racism can't simply end? Why the fears, the gears are still slowly turning?

I see the problem - like a surgeon sees a cancerous tumor, thudding inside with veins, after cutting open the skin

This is more than skin deep
It's because you have the old generation and the new generation

The new generation wants freedom for all
And acceptance, equality
Glittery idealism

It's not that the older generation doesn't want those things
But that their experiences and encounters with each other have been less glitter and more of the shitter

A fiery social media post wont fix it
But social media does fan the flames
There is no well written set of words that can put out this fire .

The Words of the Bible created the mess of hatred towards

homosexuality… All it needed was other WORDS to undo that situation.

HOWEVER. Words can't fix this problem.
Can they help locate, identify and diagnose the problem?
Yes!
But papers, social media rants, books and talk cant solve this.

It's outside the domain of the collegiate and wannabe intellectual.

It's a problem that cant be squared away, only intellectually.

It's about human experience and the ridges of the human brain drying
and becoming set in stubbornness denial and deflection

I must my run my fingers across those soft pink, squishy ridges

Holds the brain of someone who used to be living up to the class

Guess which skin color they were???

Squishes the brain, slightly

The class yells white people, some yell black people

Waits a second

NEITHER! THIS IS FROM CHINA AND HE DIED FROM COVID

Slabs the Brain onto the tray and begins the lecture

Black people and white people have been awful to each other

How a race of much smaller dicked men managed to enslave sell and
own bigger dicked men as property is a strange historical oddity

It's honestly humorous if their wasn't so much pain behind the fact
Generational divides and wounds passed down from person to child

Resentment on both sides
Black people not understanding why they are targeted
White people fearing blacks

The stereotype has power
More power than black power
More power than white power
The stereotypes are human power
To the cruel road of justification
Even when it's unjustified

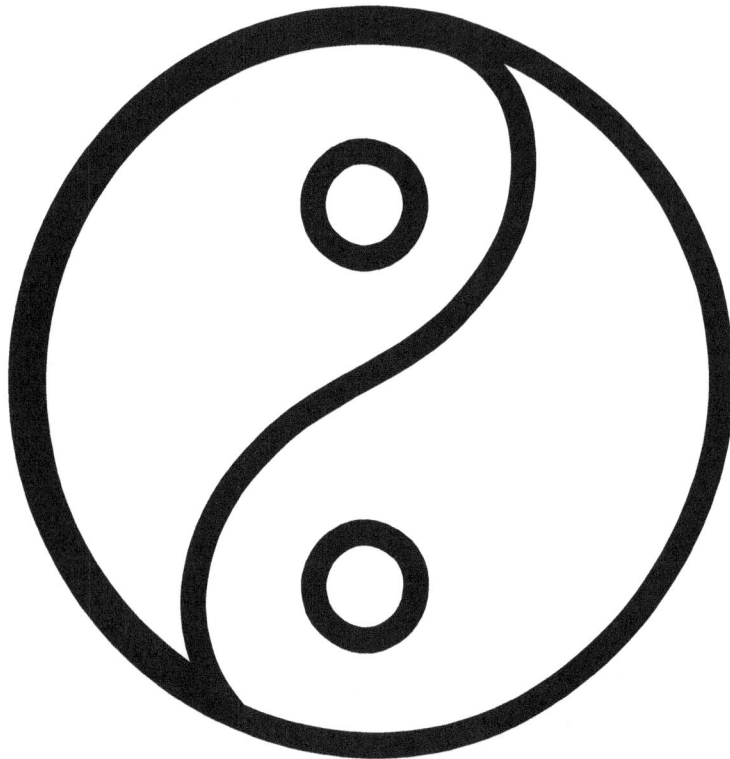

Black ink
White page

Black soul
White skin

White soul
Black skin

White lies
Black eyes

White out
~~Black out~~

Black lives
White wives

White guys
Black ties

Black People
White Thinking

White People
Black Thinking

Black and White
Black and White
Black and White
Black and White

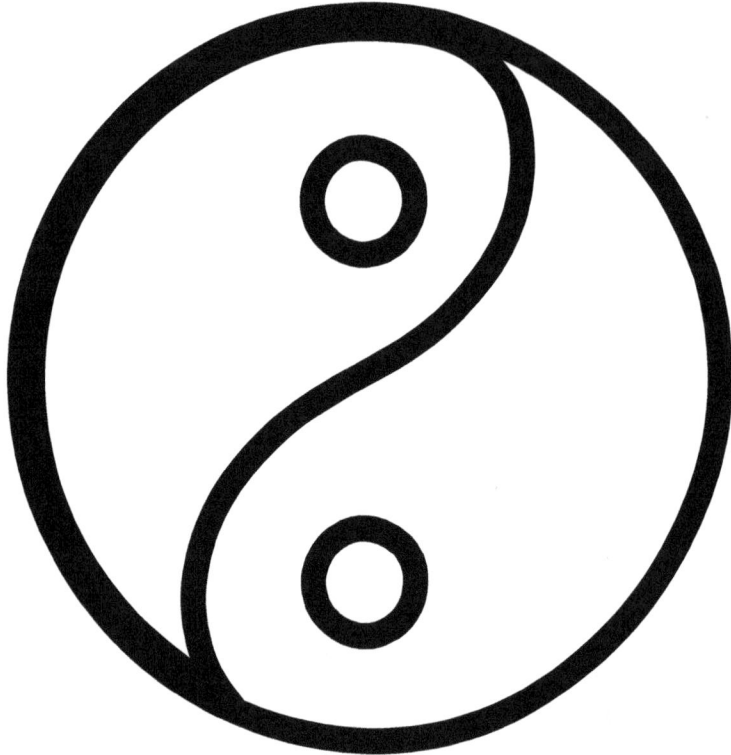

Where is the color?
Colored People
Langston HUES
Racial hatred gives me the blues
Besides Corona, It's the only thing currently in the news

NEWS FLASH:
WHEN IT'S
All or nothing
and
When all go in two different directions
Nothing changes

Like the Chinese Finger Toy,
The **harder both parties** go the other way,
the **tighter it constricts,**
You can only remove it,
and Solve the problem,
By **coming together.**

Lincoln Knew It.
A house divided cannot stand -
A White house, misguided,
with beliefs so one-sided -
Should not rule this land.

Old white lady
Starts talking to me about George Floyd
Oh god I thought
Here we go

I already KNEW what she was gonna say
"Well, u know… they found drugs in his system… she quietly tapers off,
as if that justifies his death along with all the black people killed, unjustly.

Lemme say this once, and never again.

The cops - THE POLICE - are not judge, jury, and executioner.

Even IF a person is in VIOLATION of the law,
that does not MEAN, that the law gets to just sentence them to death ON
THE SPOT - that's the very basis of the DUE PROCESS of the judicial
system of the United States.

Unless someone is putting another person in immediate peril, or acting in
obvious self defense, NOBODY, not the cops, not me, not you, not YO
MAMA, should be out here killing people.

You don't sit on someones neck for MINUTES when the most they did
was have a fake twenty dollar bill?????

BECKY, WHAT.

Everyone should be outraged at that.
If your white uncle Cleetus had been killed out on his farm, by an officer
sitting on his neck, while he begged for help because he forgot to park
his tractor, correctly, you know DAMN well Aunt June would have been
down at the county station raising hell and going BALLISTIC

So.

I get it
I fucking get it

I was outraged at 18
When school newspaper
Said all gays were deviants who slept around
And I was so mad because that wasn't ME

So I get it. I totally understand
I had to contend with the weight of lies
Falsehoods and stereotypes
And the anger made me lash out severely
At the people who kept repeating more lies

**Here's the thing - of what all this comes
down to -**

Dear white people,
Are ü listening?

Black people are **telling ü** they are tired

of this same old shit

They don't want to be treated like second
class

They don't want to be looked down on

Whether you agree with the protests and
tearing down statues or not
Whether you agree with the pathway

The road they are currently walking is **saying** loud and clear

No more

Dear black people,
You probably won't listen but here's the most honest thing I could ever say

There are <u>real issues within</u> your home base that need to be addressed
And only one thing can be addressed at a time
But somewhere down the road you've got to handle your business on this
And though you may think it's "none of my business"

After all the black guys I dated and got close to, the closest you can get to another person in this life, **the same set of issues** cropped up

I'm not even going to spell out those issues
or try and be delicate explaining what they
are, because we both already know what

those issues are

If it's black and white thinking, it won't solve
these problems
If it's black and white people, it will require
coming together
Not pulling apart

We're not going back to the civil war days
Of soldiers lying in a field, dying in agony
Near each other
And black people cooking in a kitchen

In a weird way, back then it was white people
fighting other white people
About what to do with black people

And that element hasn't changed

Society is going to have to simply put up with this uncomfortable tension as it resolves itself, flairs back up, the old arguments and wounds taken out, in different forms, until it fixes itself

And ult8mately it will, but it's going to be a

process

First it was slavery, THEN it was segregation, Now it's the understanding the black lives

matter

This is the third concussive historical wave erupting through the ground like a racial

earthquake

SO.
Let the pillars and cabinets of this house
wobble, violently,
If that's what it takes

HOWEVER,
COWEVER
??

The scorpio is about to jump out

You touch me OR my property - and I don't care what race, what sexuality, what nationality, what Indian experimental religion, I don't give a DAMN if god himself does it - the only thing going down in flames will be YOU and not my building. I'm not a giant corporation like target, I don't have safety to recuperate a loss. Y'all are gonna find out that people aren't gonna agree with you wanting to let others destroy their assets to stay alive in America, and I don't give a flying gay goat how many times you post trying to pressure me into agreeing - I'm Not gonna. Mayhem is mayhem and not social justice no matter how righteous the misplaced anger is. I'm getting armed after this, and you're gonna find out I may not be the nice, sweet, loveable Tyler ü thought you knew. I ain't putting up with all this horse shit/unicorn piss. I'm gonna protect what's mine and if you really think you're gonna infringe upon that, I'm gonna get you gone out of my life real fast. *BANG BANG, BABY* I came from the poorhouse and I ain't going back. Everything I got, I had to claw my way up to get. Human nature is ugly as hell and I ain't playin around with this kind of nonsense. Keep trying to push this agenda down my throat, acting like I'm gonna be "oh cool, go ahead and burn down my stuff, no problem." You put a finger on me or my hard earned belongings and it's game over for ü. I ain't soft and sweet like y'all, wanna-be social justice "warriors." L OH L.

 This isn't about police brutality and reform at this point, it's just about people wanting to be giant dicks to each other under the guise of justice. I don't give a DAMN about anyone's skiN color but I will tell you I don't trust the character of about 75% people out here of all shades. Your morals and actions are that of a human dumpster - here's the real news flash - I love y'all, but I don't NEED y'all. So go ahead and take that social media door lmao. ??????Truth is people barely tolerate each other and that love doesn't extend very deep. Reputation is a shifting entity, at any given second people can fall out with each other. ??????I got about five times more brass to stand up for what's right even when it's not popular, and creates friction - my opinions and fixed stances aren't formed by the lousy echo chamber of other people. Y'all need ten likes and communal support to feel validated, I ain't weak like #that. I'm about too damn real for format anyway. I don't agree with you and I don't have to lmao. Wrong is wrong. IF you think it's acceptable to torch AND Steal other people's stuff, then….. (I don't even have to think twice about saying this one)…. I don't want your corrupt ass near me then anyway

BITCH.

Shopped At Half Price Books, Now Sold There

Shopped at Barnes and Noble, now Carried There

Dropped out of College with No Creative Writing Degree

Published Ten Years Later

Told I would never sell any books

Sold Across the Globe.

YING YANG

TELL ME THE BIGGEST DOUBLE RIDDLE OF THEM ALL:

WHY DOES A MAN'S **DARKEST** THOUGHTS.....

PRODUCE HIS WHITEST SEXUAL FLUID

THE END OF DUALITY/LER

Sees my first black boyfriend,

I see two kids - from separate racial backgrounds - holding hands

I see us becoming teens and making out inside a Forest

I see us making love in the dark, while our friends were playing hide and seek

Time speeds up

I see him yelling at me that he isn't gay,
I see me with my face in my hands

I remember the shame, the confusion

I can hear him saying

"If anyone found out,
I would be ruined for life."

This stays between me and you, he says

I see culture, religion, race, family, and people
pulling us apart.

Forever.

From Book One To Book 4:

I had an easier time talking about the flames of hell /
Than I did discussing the fiery words + tear drops of race.

它来自我们
It came from us

我们做到了

We did this

它来自中国
It came from The Motherland

它杀死了肺
It kills the lungs

我们知道是谁做的
We know who did it

互相打架
Fight Each Other Now

只有中国才重要
Only China and Chinese Life Matters

中国第一，美国可能受苦
China First, America May Suffer

让白人和黑人互相残杀
Let white and black kill each other

通过谎言，我们变得更强大
Through Lies, We Become Stronger

中国共产党
Communist Party of China

永远的共产主义，民主不会持久

Forever communism, democracy will not last

毒药从东方蔓延
Poison spread from the east

再见自由女神
Goodbye, Lady Liberty

她死于咳嗽
Look as She falls down to her death, coughing

胜利
Victory

FIRECRACKER

Born on
George
Washington's
Birthday,
Must I also wear the
mantle of his

legacy?

To Be or Not To Be?
.. To be Continued.

BONUS CONTENT

Bonus:

But with alllllllllllll that being said, I can tell ü FROM firsthand experience that white people arent comfortable with things that aren't VISUALLY white.
I tanned for years and took so much crap from only other white peoples for it
If you aren't the same shade of pasty and wintery as them, they get uncomfortable and try and probe into your appearance
I took a million shots from others at my appearance

Why are you so tan

Why do you look like that
Why are you orange

Super blunt rude questions
That by the end, didn't even make me flinch

Because I wanted to, because I could
Not because I was trying to be black
But simply because glowing a color besides WHITE made me look healthy, alive
and ready for the day

I eventually moved to liquid foundations and makeup but oh MY GOD the level of
hysteria I took from white peoples

Honestly white people being so rude for so long to me about my image
Made me stop being self conscious at all

It's hard to make me feel weird or conscious of my appearance anymore
So thank you, to all the dickhead likely racist whites out there who want
everything and everyone to be white

This book is for ü lmao

I think that's the thing
Y'all act like the white tribe is this loving and accepting group to their own

These bitches have given me the third degree since I got down here
So y'all thinking I have some deep love for the white community
Hell I don't even have love for the gay community

Some of y'all need to reconsider the parameters that you judge others by
because they are wildly off base

Maybe

**Whites privilege isn't about being poor, while that's true in DEGREES,
being ostracized for a lack of wealth from others of the exact same skin**

color is ....

Lemme just tell y'all something ABOUT white people

They look down - despite going to church - and claiming they love everyone, but there are huge segments of the white population so snooty and enthralled by their own financial status that anyone else that doesn't match that income bracket is seen as inferior, but it's never said, you can just tell it in their attitude

For example, in my own city there is another city called ******* where they all act like giant dickheads because of their modest wealth. We're not even talking about true rich people, we're talking about just the upper middle class.

Lmao. They are BARELY upper middle class.

+ Jerks, is putting it nicely!

Go fifty miles outside these white cities and nobody has a clue who they are, but they act like they are the privileged SNAPCHAT kings and queens of the ENTIRE state.

Being poor and white and not experiencing that side of the tracks and not having an financial scholarships or awards that I qualified for even tho I scored higher over my friends whose racial minority status qualified them for grants that gave full rides out to school

Second of all, that church shit doesn't mean jack shit.

All that sermon goes into one ear and out the other come lunch time when they run to a restaurant and act like pigs

Y'all perceive it as simply just white vs black and it's more like white on white vs white vs white

Hell even the black community does the same exact shit to mixed people

They aren't black enough, they are too white, they are too whatever

Y'all gonna understand something

The hierarchy is everywhere, in every system, structure, building, organization, group, ethnicity, minority, majority.

It simply means, someone is having an amazing time while someone else is having a shitty time

While strutting through the streets y'all acting like it's white utopia out here

White people hate the living fuck out of other whites

It's not as clear cut as people think it is

It seems homogenous from a distance, but up close, and you learn of the alliances, disdain, hatred, secret feuds, bitter conflicts kept private that people have with each other and that shits for white people, black people and all people

People are seriously screwed up out here but it's all kept hidden by the smiles and surface level interactions

Y'all act like white people dont kill divorce cheat and fuck each other over

The honest to god truth is | people do some seriously awful psychological and emotional stuff to each other
down on this planet

I think of my best friend who sat with me at lunch - in the library - because I was sick of everyone's shit.
She was black and it never mattered, we kept each other company to pass time, everyday,

I think of the black guys I fell for, when I said "I Love U"
It wasn't the skin, of either of, that made a difference,
It was what was inside.

I think of every human interaction, I ever had.

I think of kissing another guy, hidden away from this ugly, hateful world, and my heart splitting open into music notes
as I felt a hand touch mine.

As he ejaculated, and quietly moaned he loved me -

you know what didn't matter in that moment.
counts off fingers

- ✓ THE BIBLE DIDNT MATTER
- ✓ THE STUPID ASS VERSES FROM LEVITICUS DIDNT FUCKIN MATTER
- ✓ HIS **SKIN COLOR** DIDNT MATTER
- ✓ WHAT PEOPLE WOULD SAY OR THINK DIDNT MATTER
- ✓ HOW PEOPLE WOULD FEEL AND TALK IF THEY KNEW - ALSO DIDNT MATTER

You know what mattered in THAT moment?

Our lives

mattered.

And the man I loved,
pulling me to him,
and NOT a Godamn Thing else BESIDES that.

The Fucking End, Motha-Fuckas.
4 books written in ONE year, CLAP YA HANDS MOTH=A=FUCKAS!!!

NOW --- ON REPARATIONS:

The Cable Company can BARELY get their hundred dollars out of me - and that's
in the actual here and now -
If you really think, you're going to get a check out of me, for something back
THEN…. hundreds of years gone by

laughs

I barely will pay for something I willingly DO use and have consciously utilized (Cable is an innocent service, slavery was not)

But you think Ill actually pony up reparation money for something I didn't do, support or even use????

I ain't paying for that **#$hit.**

cuz I didn't #Do #Cause #Enable or #Endorse that #Shit.

And #That's #That About **#That.**

www.ingramcontent.com/pod-product-compliance
Lightning Source LLC
Chambersburg PA
CBHW081722270326
41933CB00017B/3256